Authors' Note

Welcome to our Spriggles family! Spriggles combines "spirit" and "giggles" to motivate young children to lead healthy, active, and enthusiastic lifestyles.

It is important to recognize that while being colorful, playful, and fun, "Spriggles Motivational Books for Children" are, above all else, interactive and educational tools. These are books to be read together by parents and children, grandparents and children, educators and children, and anyone else with a sincere concern for the emotional direction of our kids. As interactive tools, these books enable us to reinforce the positive messages contained on every page. When we read "Eat a balanced meal, Seal," it's an ideal time to explain to a child the importance of selecting food sources that provide the proper balance of vitamins and nutrients. As well, when we read "Take a bath, Giraffe," it's an ideal time to explain the concept of proper hygiene, and then reinforce it with "Shampoo your hair, Grizzly Bear," and "Scrub between your toes, Crows."

As educational tools, these books will increase a child's vocabulary with words such as "healthy," "active," and "energy," while developing and enhancing their recognition of many different animals. We understand that a few of the words may be above the level of the younger children, but the illustrations and rhymes are sure to delight them. As these children age and their intellect develops, the stories and messages that accompany the illustrations will have a lasting effect as long as they are taught and reinforced. Please feel free to contact us at (888) 875-5856 or visit our website at www.spriggles.com if you desire further assistance with any of the concepts presented in these books.

And remember, we as parents, grandparents, educators, and anyone else reading these stories are never beyond needing a little motivation ourselves. So go ahead and sneak a peek when you need a reminder to "Develop good habits, Rabbits" or "Limit the fat, Cat."

Better yet, have the kids remind you!

When Stanley Seal eats all the right foods, he has lots of energy and stays healthy.

So what do we tell Stanley?

"Eat a balanced meal, Seal"

Mindy Mink knows she should drink even before she gets thirsty and wonders what drink is best for her.

So what do we tell Mindy?

"Have lots of water to drink, Mink"

When Jack Yak gets hungry between meals he eats foods that are good for him.

So what do we tell Jack?

"Have a healthy snack, Yak"

Polly Parakeet teaches her children
that one piece of candy is all right,
but too many may make them sick.

So what do we
tell Polly's kids?

HAPPY HALLOWEEN

"Go easy on the sweets, Parakeets"

Molly Moose starts her day with a big glass of fresh juice.

So what do we tell jolly Molly?

"Squeeze some juice, Moose"

Kiley Copperhead wants to have strong teeth and a bright smile.

So what do we tell smiley Kiley?

"Brush before bed, Copperhead"

Al Albatross wants his gums to stay pink and healthy.

So what do we tell our pal Al?

"Remember to floss, Albatross"

Carter Cat loves ice cream and chips, but he knows there are foods that taste just as good and have less fat.

So what do we tell smarter Carter?

"Limit the fat, Cat"

Marvin Mule is so busy doing homework, riding his bike, and playing outdoors that he needs to fill his hungry body to keep his energy up.

So what do we tell starvin' Marvin?

"Be sure to re-fuel, Mule"

Frankie Flamingo likes to keep track of how tall
he's getting. Someday he wants to be just
as tall as his mommy and daddy.

So what do we
tell Frankie?

"Watch yourself grow, Flamingo"

Jason Giraffe gets very dirty when he plays outside with his friends.

So what do we tell Jason?

"Take a bath, Giraffe"

Darryl Deer gets dirty in the oddest places after a day of running and playing in the woods.

So what do we tell Darryl?

"Wash behind your ears, Deer"

It's important to eat a variety of fresh vegetables to stay healthy and active. Raw and cooked vegetables are good sources of vitamins, minerals, and fiber which help you stay strong.

So what do we tell our Spriggles friends?

"Try a carrot, Parrot"

"Nibble some corn, Bighorn"

"Have some peas, Chimpanzees"

"Eat a beet, Parakeet"

Like vegetables, fruits supply important vitamins, minerals, and fiber.
They make a great snack or dessert because they taste so sweet.

So what do we tell our Spriggles friends?

"Eat your cantaloupe, Antelope"

"Have a grape, Ape"

"Try some honeydew, Kangaroo"

"Snack on a fig, Pig"   "Peel a grapefruit, Newt"

Eddie Eel knows it's important to get a checkup so the doctor can see if everything is all right.

So what do we tell Eddie?

"Good health is ideal, Eel"

Nancy Nightingale and her family know the importance of good grooming.

So what do we tell fancy Nancy?

"Clean your nails, Nightingales"

Colette Crow knows there are lots
of places for dirt to hide
on her children.

So what do we tell
Colette and her kids?

SOAP

"Scrub between your toes, Crows"

Teri Termite takes big bites of food and
then has trouble swallowing all of it.

So what do we
tell Teri?

"Take small bites, Termites"

Gary Gazelle knows that if he doesn't chew his food it won't digest easily.

So what do we tell Gary?

"Chew your food well, Gazelle"

Rachel Rabbit knows there are some things she must keep doing to stay strong, healthy, and alert.

So what do we tell Rachel?

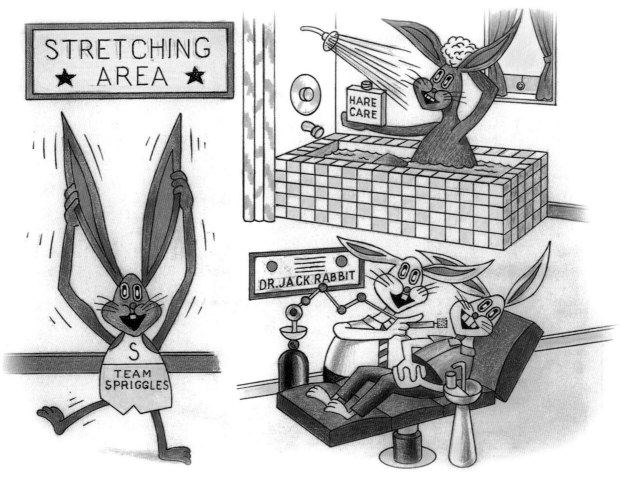

"Develop good habits, Rabbits"

Bart Buffalo takes his time when he eats.
That way his stomach lets him know
when he's had enough.

So what do we
tell smart Bart?

"Eat slow, Buffalo"

Suzy Skunk has a lot of choices when she goes to the market.

So what do we tell choosy Suzy?

"Skip the junk, Skunk"

Greta Grizzly Bear has fun playing in the river all day, but it makes her hair messy and dirty.

So what do we tell Greta?

"Shampoo your hair, Grizzly Bear"

Lucy Llama likes her children to
wear clean clothes to bed.

So what do we
tell mama's llamas?

"Wear clean pajamas, Llamas"

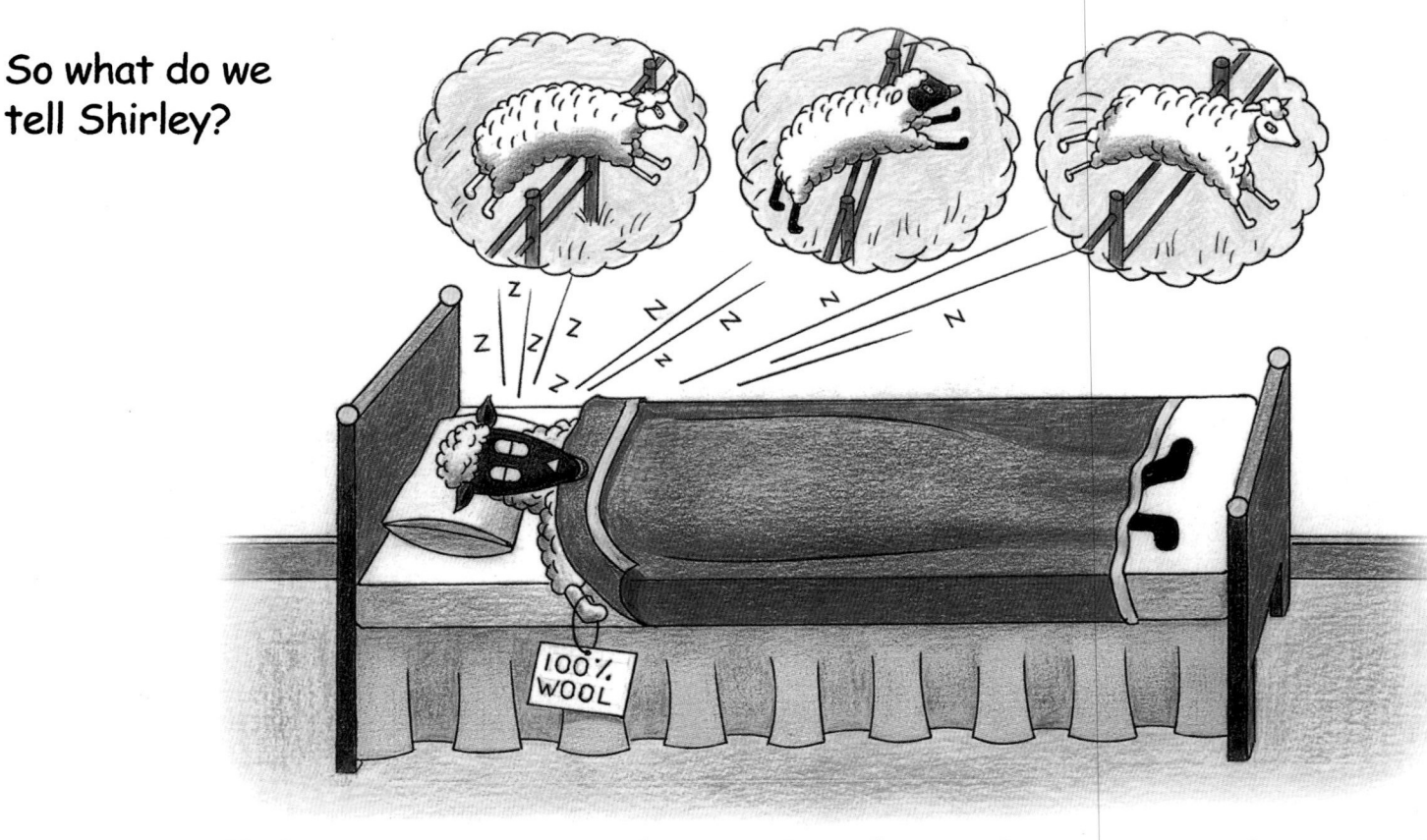